P9-CBC-434

We have . . .

NONE!

Let's pick apples
in the sun.
This looks good!

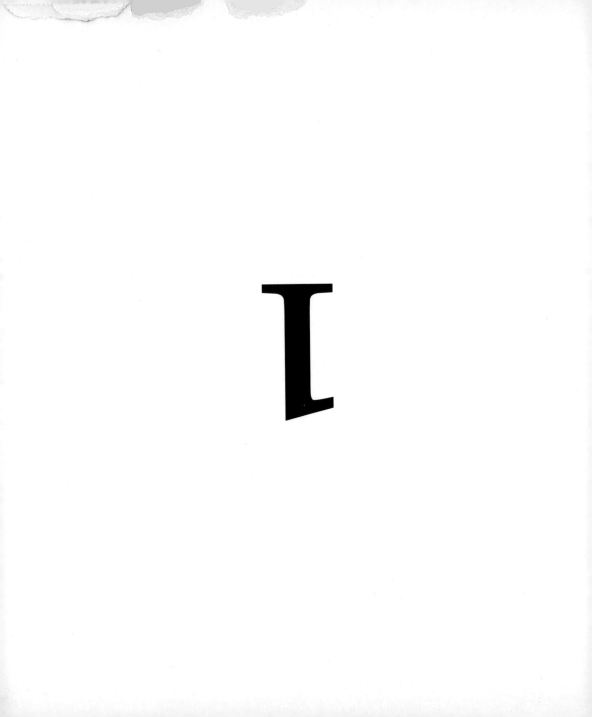

I

So high up, what should we do? Knock it down!

Now we have . . .

Let's pick that one from the tree. Lift me up!

Now we have . . .

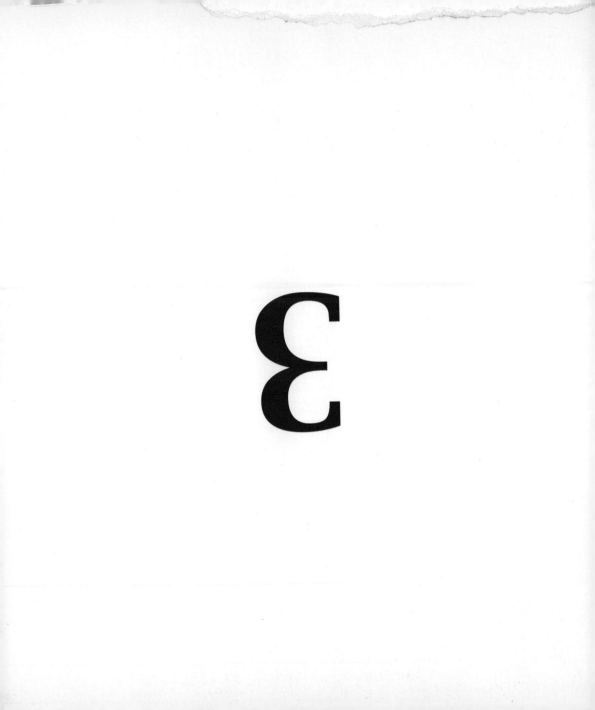

Reach and stretch to grab one more. Look in the basket

The last one comes
as a surprise—
it falls by itself!

Now we have . . .